But there has been a change in tone. The delightful escape to this romantic world is now seen as a flight from those that the poet loves and though the old-new world continues to enthrall him, Chapter One of the new volume is significantly entitled "Guilt-throes" and the very last poem in the volume is entitled "Pan Damned." The tone grows relentlessly penitential as the speaker's moods vary and the scene shifts from one aspect of the fascinating land to another.

One looks forward to the transitional Volume Two of the Trilogy, *Disappearing in Mississippi Latitudes*, to see what it will have to say about those forces that, in this concluding volume, have brought about the poet's disillusionment and ultimate decline.

— Cleanth Brooks
author of *Understanding Poetry* and
William Faulkner: The Yoknapatawpha Country

Louis Daniel Brodsky was born in St. Louis, Missouri, in 1941, where he attended St. Louis Country Day School. After earning a B.A., Magna Cum Laude, at Yale University in 1963, he received an M.A. in English from Washington University in 1967 and an M.A. in Creative Writing from San Francisco State University the following year.

From 1968 until 1987, while maintaining his poetry writing schedule, he managed a 350-person men's clothing factory and developed a chain of "Slack Outlets" for Biltwell Co., Inc. of St. Louis, Missouri.

Mr. Brodsky is the author of seventeen volumes of poetry. In addition, he has published nine scholarly books on Nobel laureate William Faulkner and, most recently, a biography titled *William Faulkner, Life Glimpses*.

Photo by Paul Lueders

Louis Daniel Brodsky

MISTRESS MISSISSIPPI

VOLUME THREE of
A MISSISSIPPI TRILOGY

Books By
LOUIS DANIEL BRODSKY

Poetry

Trilogy: A Birth Cycle (1974)
Monday's Child (1975)
The Kingdom of Gewgaw (1976)
Point of Americas II (1976)
Preparing for Incarnations (1976)
La Preciosa (1977)
Stranded in the Land of Transients (1978)
The Uncelebrated Ceremony of Pants Factory Fatso (1978)
Birds in Passage (1980)
Résumé of a Scrapegoat (1980)
Mississippi Vistas: Volume One
   of *A Mississippi Trilogy* (1983) (1990)
You Can't Go Back, Exactly (1988)
The Thorough Earth (1989)
Four and Twenty Blackbirds Soaring (1989)
Falling from Heaven: Holocaust Poems of a Jew
   and a Gentile (with William Heyen) (1991)
Forever, for Now: Poems for a Later Love (1991)

Bibliography (Co-authored with Robert W. Hamblin)

Selections from the William Faulkner Collection of
   Louis Daniel Brodsky: A Descriptive Catalogue (1979)

Faulkner: A Comprehensive Guide to the Brodsky Collection
   Volume I: The Biobibliography (1982)
   Volume II: The Letters (1984)
   Volume III: The De Gaulle Story (1984)
   Volume IV: Battle Cry (1985)
   Volume V: Manuscripts and Documents (1989)

Country Lawyer and Other Stories for the Screen by
   William Faulkner (1987)

Stallion Road: A Screenplay by William Faulkner (1989)

Biography

William Faulkner, Life Glimpses (1990)

MISTRESS MISSISSIPPI

VOLUME THREE of
A MISSISSIPPI TRILOGY

Poems by
Louis Daniel Brodsky

Louis Daniel Brodsky
12/28/07
St. Louis, MO

TIME BEING BOOKS
POETRY IN SIGHT AND SOUND
Saint Louis, Missouri

Time Being Books
10411 Clayton Road
Saint Louis, Missouri 63131

Time Being Books volumes are printed on acid-free paper, and binding materials are chosen for strength and durability.

Library of Congress Catalog Card Number: 90-72139

ISBN 1-877770-36-1
ISBN 1-877770-37-X (pbk.)
ISBN 1-877770-39-6 (tape)

Designed by Ruth A. Dambach
Southeast Missouri State University
Manufactured in the United States of America

First Edition, first printing (January 1992)

My gratitude and appreciation go to:

Malcolm Cowley and Lewis P. Simpson,
who in 1985 made suggestions that led to a
radical tightening of the focus of this book
and recasting of its dramatis personae;

Jane Goldberg, Editor in Chief of Time
Being Books, ever the perfectionist in matters
of diction, whose structural assessment of
Mistress Mississippi also has helped improve
its narrative development within chapters as
well as in overall design;

Jerry Call, Senior Editor of Time Being
Books, who has contributed to sharpening the
poetic sense and tuning the cadence of so
many of the poems in this volume;

Sheri Vandermolen, Time Being Book's
Assistant Editor and Archivist, who has deftly
edited the evolving versions and prepared the
setting copy of *Mistress Mississippi*;

And Ruth A. Dambach for her conscientious
eye for detail in overall design and physical
presentation of this book.

For

Cleanth Brooks
Malcolm Cowley
Lewis P. Simpson
and
Robert Penn Warren

. . . and I thought well as well him as another and then I asked him
with my eyes to ask again yes and then he asked me would I yes to
say yes my mountain flower and first I put my arms around him yes
and drew him down to me so he could feel my breasts all perfumed
yes and his heart was going like mad and yes I said yes I will Yes.

— from *Ulysses*, James Joyce

do you love him
her hand came out I didnt move it fumbled down my
arm and she held my hand flat against her chest her heart thudding
no no . . .
Caddy you hate him dont you . . .
poor Quentin . . .
. . . the honeysuckle it had got into my breathing it was on her face
and throat like paint her blood pounded against my hand I was
leaning on my other arm it began to jerk and jump and I had to pant
to get any air at all out of that thick grey honeysuckle
yes I hate him I would die for him I've already died for him I die
for him over and over again everytime this goes . . .

— from *The Sound and the Fury*, William Faulkner

. . . him there they found
Squat like a Toad, close at the ear of *Eve*;
Assaying by his Devilish art to reach
The Organs of her Fancy, . . .

— from *Paradise Lost*, John Milton

Contents

MISTRESS MISSISSIPPI

VOLUME THREE of
A MISSISSIPPI TRILOGY

Prologue

Leaving Home

I leave my sleeping wife
Undulating among seaweed and shells,
Helplessly questing for dreams to arrest,
Compress in Memory's deep grots,
Then, on waking, thread into an amulet
To be worn between her breasts forever.
She clings to the pillow
As though it were her soul mate
She's desperate to keep from straying.

Hours from this empty hour, driving south,
I'll reflect on my indifference,
How I rejected caressing her,
Expressing with a soft kiss
Pressed indelibly to her twitching lips
My guilt leaving home,
Not waking her
That she might beg me to stay,
Then I'll suppress it for the pleasures ahead.

Chapter One
GUILT-THROES

Running Scared

Rising starkly before my vision,
Mississippi's pines,
Still quite unfamiliar landmarks,
Sentinels at attention,
Invite me to press toward pleasures ahead.

They accept my presence
Without suspecting the nature of my quest.
I'm not even certain they realize
My license plates
Bear an anomalous "Show-Me" slogan

Or that my status as interloper
Invalidates my immigration papers;
They let me pass unapprehended,
Inflicting minimal paranoia.
Arkabutla Lake, Senatobia,

Hurricane Creek, the Tallahatchie River
Flash, fade, dissolve.
All the way to the Batesville-Oxford exit,
Loblolly pines
Lining both sides of I-55

Hover like trained circus bears
Standing in line on their hind legs,
Their nubby limbs tentative paws
Balancing their vast weight of sky-breeze
In my car's slipstream.

Restively I project my thoughts
On diversionary screens
(Sipping Chablis with you, Mississippi,
In naked midnight revelry)
To keep fear's monkey off my back;

➜

I let Fancy stray
From crowded metaphorical fields
Where it frequently delights in picking images
It transforms into bouquets
And places in vase-shaped poems,

Hoping to discourage my imagination
From transmuting reality
Into loblolly bears
Capable of mutilating my courage
Or chasing me out of this state of mind

Through which I drive in search of you.
Only after dusk's keeper
Locks the pines in penumbral cages
Will I relax. Perhaps someday I might relate
How close I came to quitting my Crusade.

Exhortation in Praise of Spontaneity

I'm so pleasured to meet you, Miss;
Pleased you're intrigued by me,
By what I do — that I'm a writer.
And I can promise you, Lady,
I won't expend precious energy
Spewing a ruse, weaving a spider's net
In which to snare and paralyze
An unsuspecting creature like you.

What I choose to do with my time
Is of the essence to planetary rotations,
The harmonious conjunctions of fates,
And the daily maintenance of my poet-soul.
Lady, there just ain't enough time
To squander even an integer
On dissimulation or the fabrication of facades
Just for their own selfish sakes.

My purposes are to fashion illusion from Truth
By contriving, transmuting, and fantasizing,
To make reality more palpable,
Transcend pain and depravity via metaphor,
Teach the hinged door to revolve,
Forecast unpredictable catastrophes
With absolute precision, and convince Death
To focus on ghosts, not mortal hosts.

Lady, take me as I am, or reject me
On the premise that you can't stand hyperbole
As a way of life, that poetic mode
By which we measure and appreciate
Shakespeare, Keats, and Roethke.
If you accept my outrageous expectations,
I'll translate you from words into worlds.
Otherwise, you and I will die of natural causes

→

Without discovering why Fate collaborates with Man
In creating *Gospels*, *Korans*, *Torahs*,
Tao Te Chings, and *Upanishads*.
For the moment, I implore you,
Be patient with my seemingly strange ways.
While in Xanadu, let me compose
My own Kubla Khan's closure
Before I expose you to celestial human love.

Jongleur: Initiation Rites

Slowly the membranous pseudo-closure
Succumbs to flute notes
Your first lover's tongue
Blows with fricative motion; you whimper
As the painful ecstasy of being penetrated
By that original, ephemeral exhalation,
Forever setting the valve ajar,
Quavers your spine, nipples,
And pulsating vulva.

I rest my tempestuous forehead on your chest
And listen to your impassioned pump
Thumping primitive pulses
Like a blood-flood cresting incessantly
Beneath the surface of the River Earth.
You wet my dry lips with your tongue,
Run one finger around the mouthpiece
Behind which silent poems await release
As if to spring me free

So that in repose you might know,
As you did during your birth
Into the Dominion of Relinquished Virginity,
Your supple, newly initiated maidenhood,
Stored in glands and cells
Impregnable except by desire,
Will still elicit my voluptuous music.
Soon you'll compose yourself
For the coda I'll write — Satan's epithalamium.

Guilt-throes

And now, all that anticipation
Splinters into fragments of bafflement and wonder
About how and why
Time can cast sinister shadows
Over aspirations we claim as our own
In the name of love, change, and wisdom
And alchemize twilight into its base obscurity.

Ah, that perpetual, immutable plaint
Writ by the bard, by Marvell,
Keats, myriad laureates, and by me
Whenever recreating the vessel
In which to bury an old lament or recent grief:
Each poem caskets the ashes and bones
We consecrate to blind and illusory immortality

By conjuring, scheming how to outwit,
With mere syllables and rhymes, Obliteration.
Yet none has ever discovered,
Even through necromancy or demonology,
How to materialize djinn-like
Whenever lovers stroke the instrument gently
With recitations suffused with empathy and awe.

Suddenly, having waited such a long time
Before sacrificing my integrity, dear Lady,
Submitting physically to someone
Too smooth, youthful, and bemused
By the newness of possessing an unfantasized man
To suspect the Devil of conspiring with Fate,
I've discovered the intimate shape of empty space.

Lady of Fiesole

Once again empty self-centeredness —
Silence so wide
Day and night are indistinguishable —
Violates me, vitiates all ties with today,
Rendering yesterday as irredeemable
As an expired pass to the gates of Hippocrene;
Transmogrification is imminent.

Mile after mile,
Your gentle visage rises before me
In sinuous, Beardsleyesque reiteration,
Voiceless yet murmurous as seeds
Stirring beneath seething earth,
Waiting to burst and blossom
Into a virgin's first and final lament.

But my eyes are blind to your keening;
My ears perceive only silhouettes
On shimmering afternoon's scrim curtain.
Nothing is certain
Except that your image continues to recede
Despite frequencies I keep adjusting
In hope of reconnecting with your echo.

Abruptly, mirages cease.
Neither of us exists; we never have.
For that matter, fantasies,
Weighted with possibilities of touching someone
Whose future you might possess,
Refuse to relinquish their clairvoyance.
Like a tidal wave unleashed in Hades,

The widening silence sideswipes my vessel.
Heaved overboard, I float face down,
Unable to breathe or drown,
Then yield to intermittent comas, to sleep.
Suddenly, through the viscid, liquid distance,
You swim into my eyes
To guide me back to dreaming's Fiesole.

Defrocked

Having stopped on this headlong trek home,
This raucous juggernaut
Out of honeyed Canaan,
To replenish the caffeine
Streaming through my artificially excited system,
I now resume the final leg,
Hoping to make an inconspicuous approach
And unscandalous landing.

Neurotically reviewing calculations,
Statistical figures,
In case my delay warrants justification,
I rehearse viable scenarios and alibis,
Fabricate convenient obstacles
That could have threatened my safety,
Caused sufficient consternation
To keep me from leaving Oxford sooner.

Although driving I-55
For six consecutive hours,
I, a migrating aviator, fly low,
Going north into colder and colder climes:
As I enter the geography
That spawned my profound distaste for mediocrity
And bland ambitions,
My eyes recognize not one familiar sign;

Instead, my ears clog,
And my stomach knots;
Vision is an asthmatic attack;
This malaise, accompanied by fear
That these grievous symptoms
Are an occupational hazard of existence
In New Laputa and St. Louis,
Announces my presence in the old air zone.

Now, cruising downwind to my house,
Surveying the land-lay,
My ears detect an urgent groaning
Emanating from the engine.
Five miles out, I lose full power,
Slide into a steep dive,
And, jettisoning my wits,
Forgetting all emergency procedures, crash.
Anesthetized from Chablis vapors
My shattered visage requires to stay alive,
I mumble salutations
And feigned sighs of relief to my wife,
Preoccupy my greeting with needless details
About my mission to the hinterland,
My Crusade to Mecca to proselytize devotees,
And pray loquacious dreams won't expose my apostasy.

Chapter Two
A RENEWAL OF FAITH

A Renewal of Faith

Tracking south in my fleet vehicle,
I whisper past a green and white sign
Proclaiming Wilson and Lepanto,
Cruise under viaducts,
Approaching mile by minute Belle Memphis,
That, as yet, unseen ghostly Lady,
And hurl recklessly toward the River.

Whether seeking absolution
In Beulahland's baptismal stream
Or crusading to a Canaan south of Eden
Remains for me to ascertain.
Already my flesh quivers and itches
As if I were sinking in quicksand,
Naked, unable to scream for extrication.

Signs for Tyronza and Jericho
Remind me I'm yet enslaved by Arkansas
And may not reach Mississippi even by dusk.
But my apostate heart has faith
You'll be waiting in Oxford to jog with me
Through sultry Bailey's Woods
And inspire my drowning soul with your buoyancy.

Poetic Vectoring

Entering you, Mississippi, of my own volition,
My ears hear in the distance
Your whisperous voice
Redeeming from desperation and loneliness
My decision to leave home again.

My eyes strain to locate the source
From which your transmissions emanate;
Imagination sets up vectors
My intuition selects
In plotting a flight plan and landing,

Yet my guidance systems
Fail to focus your elusive shape
On the eyes' screens.
I wait for omens, totems,
Superstitious rituals to signal your existence

In this mystical airspace
Three hundred thirty-three miles due south,
Inviting me to climb high
Into your tree house,
Rest from my clandestine odyssey,

Sip chilled Chablis, kiss warm lips,
And get celestially blitzed.
After a statical lapse,
I catch sight of your voice
Racing nakedly again across my wrist,

Making my phoenix-quill pen
Compose your heart's verse,
Guiding me to St. Peter's Cemetery
On a frequency your inspiration creates
As you sing me softly "home" within my poem.

Collision Course

Singing winds bring me "home"
On wings thoughts of you buoy;
Their heather-hued plumage
Is your exquisite, naked shape
Stippling Memory's orange-pink horizon.

Flying toward you in Metaphor's fuselage
As you penetrate my sector
Aboard your Brancusi-sleek sky-seal,
Inexorably converging on colliding vectors,
My unchecked recklessness crescendos.

Soon, released from holding patterns
We've negotiated too long
For the tight scheduling of migrating souls,
We'll make our go-around and, landing in tandem,
Soar again into silence, climaxing.

Garden of Southern Delights

Lady, since last we spent gentle energies
Contriving affectionate devices
To command each other's attentions,
I've experienced a friendless dereliction.

Sweet Mistress, until this Sunday morning,
When again I entered your misty provinces,
I'd forgotten just how much time
We've wasted not stitching our illicit crazy-quilt.

Now, racing past Hurricane Creek, Como,
Approximating Oxford after nearly a year,
I sense your deliquescent fragrance
Of magnolia, wisteria, and honeysuckle.

Soon, surreptitiously,
We'll meet in Bailey's Woods
And, suspending all that's transpired since then,
Let silence put us in touch with our future,

Set us free from the past,
And remand us to mutual jubilation.
With luck, under tonight's luminous moon-bloom,
We'll exult in ageless efflorescence.

Night Vipers

Strange how each day away from you
Creates a vicious peristalsis
That knots up in my gut
Like a cobra in a croker sack
Mistaking itself for a mongoose.

For months on end, I'm its victim;
Paralyzed, I dissolve in venomous juices
Slithering night spits at me.
At home, I'm unable to eat
For nausea's perforating fangs.

Lady, if only we were tree snakes,
Green and gold, slender, gentle, sensual,
Silently side-sliding skyward
Toward our secret heat
As we are tonight in Oxford's rain forest,

We might suspend our love from Eden's limb,
Never fearing disappearance into the Abyss
That, except for these trips,
Separates our existences,
And subsist on each other's appetites.

Diana

Home again, synaptic fireflies
Illuminate daydreaming's cave
In which déjà-vu intuitions of you
Drip like icy stalactites
From Night's glistening ceiling;
Their mind-sparks undarken the space between us,

Transmute me into moonbeams
Probing the leaves shading your "tree house,"
Piercing its windows and diaphanous curtains,
Entering your fragrant chamber,
And penetrating you, rife in menstruation,
On your Dylanesque brass bed.

I ride September's lunar tides back to July,
Reach Memory's lagoon on smooth waves,
My head coming to rest
Beneath your breasts' reef.
All evening, your bleeding cleanses fantasies,
Purges demon-sleep.

Awakening at sunrise's red edge,
I witness your image dimming into an ocean
Draining into a cave
Overflowing with fireflies randomly blazing.
Standing in their reflected light,
I gaze at a full moon — it's *you* I see!

Chapter Three
SWEET RUINATION

A Gift of Time

Driving I-55 southerly,
I weave the tedious hours into a lanyard
To gift my mistress, Mississippi,
Later this rainy April afternoon
On greeting her after such a protracted absence.

I braid the subtly changing strands
With an artificer's nimble precision,
Alternating green with silver,
Silver with green, in dizzy crisscrossing
Whose susurration is the music of uprootedness.

The water's rhythmic densities,
Pelting the windshield, rising from tires,
Shimmering in the distant landscape
Filling with vernal hues
As I cruise past Sikeston toward Memphis,

Rather than confusing vision,
Appear to enhance the necromantic design
Defining itself mile by mile by mile;
The lanyard lengthens
As if I, God's artisan, were extruding it by hand.

Hour after solitudinous hour,
It continues to devour my concentration.
The closer I approach Oxford,
The more complete the woven creation becomes,
And the greater grows my anticipation

Of knotting and clipping loose ends,
Cauterizing them in a silver-green embrace
I'll place around my Lady's neck.
Soon I'll glimpse you emerging from Bailey's Woods —
You'll already know what I've brought you.

Mistress Mississippi

Traveling south out of St. Louis,
My inner Ear and inward Eye
Approximate singing, tinkling chimes
I listen to while driving the highway down,
Narrowing the miasmic miles
By hours to minutes to inches,
An infinitesimal distance
Finally separating you and me
From all the accreted silence and lonely desire
We've allowed to infiltrate lacunae
Infused in our hearts' affair.

Pressing inexorably past Cape Girardeau,
Sikeston, and Blytheville,
And after crossing the bridge into Memphis,
I finally arrive at Oxford,
Fantasy's landing your silhouette fills
With the mythos of lace-frilled Melanie,
Brocaded plantation mistress,
Possessing a lilting, yet whisperous, voice
And slender, shapely figure,
A roundelay whose deliquescent music
Subdues my veins' juices.

Lady-in-waiting, Mississippi is you —
Neither naiad, vestal virgin, nor muse
But palpable, pedestaled, naked evocation,
Fuguelike, elusive, dream-seeming
Yet real as the ecstasy your lips translate
To communicate with my seething body
Each time we achieve, simultaneously,
A spiraling, perfectly timed climax.
I and you, my sensual Delta belle,
Child of my deft conception,
Will eventually accomplish our own sweet ruination.

Though intuiting this all too well,
My intellect, nevertheless,
Refuses to deflect Destiny's direction,
Chooses instead to let us suffer the future,
A volitionless choice really
Since profligacy and Old Testament prophecy
Are so ambiguously interwoven
As to permit, at times encourage, spontaneity.
Now I've arrived; the South is my anointing.
I, trusting Isaac, sacrifice myself unto your keeping.
Lady, annihilate me shamelessly.

Sweet Ruination

I enter your house
Not as a stranger yet strangely new
To your inscrutable accouterments
Gathered from Sri Lanka, Corfu,
The Nile and Amazon, Juan-les Pins.
Why you've chosen me
Upon whom to lavish your passion
I won't know until Time translates itself
In a dozen ways and the autumnal days,
Spent in ruminative solitude,
Disclose their universal secrets.

For now, I accept this gift,
Your unconditional sharing,
As an angelic bequest;
Your mellifluous kisses,
Mad rhapsodies of our lovemaking,
Glissandi we set loose through the bloodstream,
Are precious motets we perform
In this illicit relationship of our composing.
Tonight I trust you implicitly,
Without doubts,
Free of self-conscious guilt.

And willingly I'll set you free
Whenever in desolation
Your heart cries out,
Realizing gravity calls us graveward,
As it does all terrestrial objects,
To relinquish our ineffable essences.
But this magical evening,
While I yet enfold you in heated embrace,
Let us sport, cavort,
Transcend the sweetest metaphysic liquefactions,
Defy time by holding this night back;

Let us pass through fire
Singed, scarred, but unmarked for the darkness
That hides us inside the light
Emanating from our eyes;
Let us survive trials
That would compress the future into cinders,
Kindle the past, in a last-ditch attempt
To rescue all that's been jettisoned
Or lost in the chaotic Abyss.
Now then, tender Lady,
Take me to bed,

Gentle me with your friendship
And energized sensibility.
I love you for admiring me as a poet
Capable of composing your volcanos and geysers,
Rhyming your tides' crosscurrents
And galactic disturbances,
Signifying, transposing, and recadencing
Cosmic desires your heart radiates
Each time you touch me indelibly.
Tonight, a creature seeking total appreciation,
I will myself into your sweet keeping.

The Fawns

After Edna St. Vincent Millay

To have had your acceptance
With such total and unabashed passion
Is to know always that in your absence,
Long after Memory commences,
Then lapses into desperate groping
Through dark, drafty corridors
Toward your hospitable eyes' magic forest,
There'll remain a necessary tension
Between dying and ecstasy,
Forgetting and sustaining hope
Of nesting again in your gaze,
Redefining those soft contours
We kneaded out of uncommon clay,
Recapturing that fascination
So primal and defenselessly intense.

If I'd either taken you away with me
Or, certainly worse,
Never engendered the courage
On our very first tryst in Oxford
To converge on your mesmeric radiance
And dare to rearrange the spaces in our strangeness,
It's doubtful my somnolent heart
Would have known such perfect irregularity
Or my dreams, born of chimeras,
Been transformed into soaring orient herons;
Nor, just now,
Would either of us possess
Such sweet preoccupation
With the details of our inconvenienced destinies
Or be savoring the pain of our sequestration.

Ah, but indeed, dear friend,
Ivory child of my descending years
Whom I retrieved from that forest-night
When alabaster sleep enclosed us
In enchanted twilight
And trees and lovers became one entanglement
From which neither desired extrication,
You and I must preserve and extend
Our unintentioned intimacy
Or else suffer futile recrimination
For denying ourselves one of life's pleasures.
How regrettably pathetic it will be
If either of us ever forgets
We're both dappled fawns
Of the same blessed doe.

Of Elegies and Elegies

Now, as I leave Oxford,
Weaving into silence
Through 9:00 a.m.'s unusual coolness,
Flying past kudzu and loblolly pines,
The miles dissolve like minutes
Clicking away on a time bomb;

They cycle ominously
In nonrepeating inevitabilities.
Despondently I listen to sunflowers
Peering from overgrown roadside coverts
Whisper mystical concupiscences
Inarticulately in my distancing ears.

I weep into the colossal valley
Your absence spreads before my eyes,
Mississippi.
Memories festooned with Steely Dan music,
Pouilly-Fuissé, and crisp kisses
Are shimmer-mist lifting off morning's pool.

The valley widens to an immeasurable Abyss
Echoing with the amplified roar
Each invisible tear dripping from my pen
Detonates as it hits bottom
And splits into dismal strophes
That record my lonely dissolution.

Separation is such an amorphous place.
My heart's hour is Now,
But its blood stutters, sputters, back-floods
Before making atrial escape
Into terrestrial vessels
In which, pulsating recklessly,

It tries to negotiate our precious differences,
Smooth over our unshared heritages
With caring, patience, and appreciation,
Acceptance of each other's demons,
Primitive and modern goddesses and gods,
And with prodigious artistic gifts.

All the way home I hold my breath,
Hoping my arrested motion
Might let my thoughts uncreate the miles,
Dismantle geodesic spaces
One sunflower, pine, kudzu vine at a time.
But Death won't disown its ghosts.

Wind Devils

My eyes are twin wind devils
Spinning northerly
Over a continuous field
From which my retreating memory
Has gleaned your supplest harvest,

That space, a desiccated desolation,
Whose tornadic tear-dust
Rips gaping furrows in vision's crust
And turns my grief to mud and rust
As I try to see my way clear.

Receding from you, I realize
These disturbances are neither metaphors
Nor wholly optical distortions
Caused by day's dissolution into twilight
But mortal waterspouts

Rising preternaturally
From each eye's outbound tide,
Phenomenal occurrences
Resulting from abruptly changing pressures
My overheated heart,

Freezing in reaction to sadness
Over our predetermined parting,
Inevitably creates.
While miles accrue,
I watch through binocular tunnels

As your funnel-shaped image loses focus.
Suddenly I'm one
With both sinister twisters,
Their fierce motion mine,
My vertiginous spirit just more debris

Being ferried along precariously
In arbitrary dispersion.
Slowly, home closes in on chaos;
The eyes' wildness slakes,
Changes from banshee-shouts to silence,

Finally plays itself out.
By tonight, my hemic irises and pupils
Will bathe soothingly in lukewarm routine,
And the field, a plowed solitude,
Will lie fallow until our next seeding.

Sparks Jumping the Gap

Why, when you gently squeeze your eyes,
Do I materialize
Amidst your most precious treasures,
Keepsakes of the unbought variety
Chosen meticulously
From prior lives
For unique imperfections
That illuminate rather than reduce texture
And define your sense of place
In this land of Southern pride?

Why do I arise behind your eyes
Jinni-eager to satisfy,
Press your shape into mine
Like a sculptor pouring heated bronze
From his outsized imagination
Into a mold he's fashioned by hand,
And fly into sleep's peaceable kingdom,
My body your spirit's reciprocal wing,
Your cheek resting on my chest
To keep black dogs off your head?

And why, whenever you tighten your lids,
Do I recite odes to the winds,
Fling impassioned elegies
Across the Abyss whose azimuth
Is the astigmatic out-of-roundness
Your seeing accommodates and rectifies
Just by focusing me "home,"
Bringing my colors into register,
My poetry into truer resolution
With your own intuitions?

Why, if not that yours is magic
Capable of sustaining me in our absences,
Resurrecting me from desperation
Whether sliding on Missouri ice
Or breathing Mississippi humidity.
In truth, I appreciate you not only close by
But from this inhospitable distance.
You give my invisibility vision
Whenever I sense you dreaming me alive —
And I always know when you're closing your eyes.

Chapter Four
STAR-CROSSED

Scientific Observations

Since it's a philosophical given
That my needs aren't subliminal,
Where are you this evening
When I want nothing except to be with you
For being's own sake,
Not foreplay, rationalizations,
Disquisitions citing Baptist and Hebraic precedents
To nullify heathenish hypocrisies
And guilt trips more prolifically elicited
Than biblical "begats,"
Nor sound-and-light shows
Used to illuminate spent civilizations?
Just touching would be sufficient
To let me know your love for me exists.

If you and I, Lady,
Residing in incontiguous locations,
Find that our spines form common boundaries
Uniting our neighboring states of mind,
Tectonic plates of the primate kind,
Then why,
Even when quakes occur between us,
Don't our faults converge, merge,
And make us realize that metaphysical disturbances
Aren't cosmic eruptions to be feared
But insufficiencies requiring scrutiny
For solutions only our nearness can reify?

Aubade

You're the best in bed and at letters,
A 20th-century Athena;
Your intellect insinuates my head,
Enlarges my heart's meager expectations
With energy so dynamic
My libido increases tenfold
Whenever deciphering your penned hieroglyphs,
Dying into your Keatsian tropes.

Too often we sublimate our separations,
Measure them in feet and meters, not miles,
Caesuras instead of silences between breaths.
Even now I hear myself dreaming aloud:
"Lady, you're the best in bed and at letters.
Let's keep 'in touch,' stay posted
By never letting the pet owl
Resting wide-eyed on your shoulder drowse."

Unexpected Awakening

Surfacing through swirling liquefactions,
Oceans suffused with feverish dreams
Sleep has suppressed too many hours,
My waking psyche collides with visions of you
Opaqued in the eye of a meteor shower.

Your Southern dialect, intoned with phonemes
And clipped *-eds* and *-ings*
Slipping sinuously into my inner ears,
Ignites my spine, chills my flesh with heat,
Wets desiccated head-webs,
Sears fears my spirit initially sensed
Lunging out of prolonged silence
To answer your long-distance phone call.

All too libidinously I'm in day's keeping.
You, Lady, though so faraway,
Have a-proxy-mated me with spoken words,
Translated my inarticulateness into coital shapes,
Our voices embracing inextricably.

To His Distant Mistress

After Marvell,
a loose persuasion

Jeff City, Mo., and Jackson, Miss.,
Form a wide chorus only I can intuit
This celebratory Thursday morning
As the road I drive circuitously
Invites me home to your embrace
Half a Spice Islands-day away.

Your whispering, distant voice
Draws me fluidly through the slipstream
My soft thoughts create
Alternating between state capitals
Where lawyer and writer gesticulate
Acting out briefs and odes in isolation.

I listen to your motions being adjudicated,
My poems climaxing into closure
As we fly simultaneously
All afternoon toward each other
To resume where we concluded
By picking up the loose Memphian thread,

Weaving evening into a glittering cloak
To sleep naked beneath,
Then share in wearing invisibly by day
For however long it might take
Before the robe frays
And we must separate again for a duration.

Lady, even if Time finds us in contempt
For re-citing free-verse precedents
In defense of our innocence
And sentences us to Dantesque recrimination,
We must insist our loving is no sin
Or, if so, only a misdemeanor in Libra's lights.

Following the River South

Still in Missouri, my butterfly eyes
Light on a green and white sign
Proclaiming "Memphis 109" miles
Straight down I-55.
From her omniscient, invisible position
In this hazy Southern sky,
Diana tilts my body
With such supple lustfulness
Tides in my veins and arteries change course.

Oblivious of distances, my divining rod quivers.
Ahead, surmounting river's edge,
The Peabody Hotel offers my drifter's soul
Momentary hope of resurrection.
Suddenly high noon and I converge
Somewhere between firmament and earth.
We reach flood stage; levees break.
Above the bridge I cross, a naked moon shudders;
Below, my blood flows on toward New Orleans.

Under the River's Surveillance

Imagine all those trips we've shared,
Believing ourselves incognito
For having stayed in cities and towns
Teeming with faces obscure to themselves,
Collectively related neither by mores
Nor sense of place but only by demographics
Whose skew has less to do with volition
Than gratuitous cynicism and indifference.

How naive to have accepted Fate on faith,
Assumed we could flourish
While working out equations for anonymity
Without first subjecting our hypotheses
To reasonably objective tests;
How presumptuous of our intellects
To persist without bowing to empiricism,
If not wisdom, in deducing conclusions.

The fact is, we were detected from the outset,
In St. Louis, Memphis, and New Orleans,
Our clandestine intimacies
Recorded by Old Man,
Whose ubiquitous conscience
Infuses all beings within his locus
As though his muddy flooding were blood
Slowly eroding us back to dust, to nothingness.

He's seen us in our naked posturings,
Kept watch on our passages
From state to hallucinatory state
Over whose land-fantasies he claims suzerainty.
Through the fluid lenses of hotel rooms
He's viewed us importuning a reluctant future
To embrace our sacrifice to amorality
For the privilege of sending down new roots.

How we could have missed his presence
I may never know. Even if I learn,
It won't make significant difference
Since you and I, Lady,
Were fated, sooner or later, to be found out.
Now that his omniscience has unveiled us,
We can no longer rely on nature
To disguise us or let us hide inside our love.

Star-Crossed

Before leaving Baghdad-by-the-Gulf,
We stroll again through the Vieux Carré,
You, streetwise,
Remarking for my stray gaze to focus and alchemize
Objets d'art, dazed tourists,
A sax player, and Ignatius J. Reilly,
Vending weenies from a plastic hotdog.
You amuse me by imitating anglicized phonetics
Natives mangle pronouncing streets:
Toulouse, Chartres, Dauphine;
In silliness I trill their Spanish equivalents
As we locate souvenirs for our children,
Members of our "extended family"
Who will never even meet each other.

We complete this al fresco ritual
Taking Saturday buffet on the secluded patio
At The Court of Two Sisters,
Whose eucharistic bread and wine
Consist of champagne, Mouton-Cadet,
Pâté de foie gras, bagels, croissants,
Preludes to Dionysian surfeit:
Cheeses, kiwis, melons, gelatin molds,
Salad platters, seafood filets,
Crab, shrimp, lobster, crawfish étouffée,
Beans and rice, jambalaya, gumbos,
Creole and Cajun potpourris
Steaming in stainless chafing dishes,
And pastries to dazzle a Babylonian mistress.

Now, distancing twilit New Orleans,
Skimming the Mississippi's translucent bayous
Westerly toward Baton Rouge, then north
Toward Hammond, we retreat inexorably
To separate observatories
Where we'll record the variations in alignment
Our native planets may have assumed
Since we forfeited control over their rotations
Seeking apotheosis of our fluctuating souls.
Knowing we're heading home together
Only as far as Memphis, we illumine,
Like twin shooting stars flaming across the sky,
What's left of this flight
With the heat of our hearts' sad, sweet stroking.

Mizpah

Genesis xxxi. 44-49

Gray the day, and grayer still
My resonating heart's regret
On separating yet again;
It's almost as though endings,
Not resumptions conjured in daydreams
Devoted to arresting interludes
And assigning them to sweet clandestine use,
Were Illusion's raison d'être.

I can't stand partings,
Especially when they're suspended in rain
Like this persistently grieving mist
Through which we drive out of Memphis
In opposite directions,
Diminishing our blessed nexus
To Mizpah whispers
Etched on vision's windshield.

But for mystic reasons this Saturday morning,
Just listening to the precipitation
Has privileged me, solely,
To translate revelation within revelation
Arising from circle within circle
Dispersing in light widening into light.
In its voice I hear yours beseeching,
"Let the Lord watch between me and thee."

Chapter Five
ENCOUNTERS SOUTH:
OXFORD-MEMPHIS-JACKSON

In Defense of Physical Manifestations

From Love's extremities,
Where each distinct edge of its antipodes
Rubs noiselessly against Eternity,

We rush toward Oxford,
Our passions cyclones converging urgently,
Locomotives closing on the same track.

The location of our fated clandestination
Has neither latitude nor azimuth
But rather is measured in fiery degrees

Whose mutual habitations vary
Coincidently with the erratic beat
Our sympathetic imaginations generate

Each time either contemplates trysting.
Such sweet release is both rhyme
And divine reason for this distanced longing

You, mistress, and I, your heart's bard,
Conceive as strophe, caesura, and closure
Whenever we sing the universe awake.

Soon we'll blend our voices again
In seminal remembrance
And harmonize all verses deleted from Genesis

(An orgasmic catechism), hoping poetry,
The body's metaphysical apotheosis,
Will recovenant us with God.

Skimming Mississippi's Rim

Surreptitiously we leave Oxford,
Fleeing previously separate identities
Fused now despite driving to Memphis
In vehicles bearing "Show-Me"
And "The Magnolia State" plates.
We share a collective freedom
Our recent lovemaking
Licenses us to perpetuate indefinitely,
Provided we continue respecting its ukase:
In matters of human appreciation,
Possession is only *one-tenth* of the Law.

Ahead of mine, your fleet white car
Weaves through I-55's flow
As the Tallahatchie, Como, and Senatobia
Slide behind pine-paled fortresses.
Witnessing you from this oblique distance
Starts vision wondering
Whether we might not be Keatsian children
Indeterminately stranded
On an urn whose rim girds our life spans.
Ah, but then, on a day so premeditated,
Why surrender to the poetic?

The Peabody

Indeed, David Cohn may hold copyright
To the prosaic trope that the Delta begins
In the lobby of the Peabody Hotel,
But, in perpetuity,
I possess poetic title to Tennessee
Deeded me last evening
In room 1163
Of that Memphian Versailles
Where, partaking of pagan eucharist,
Our hearts consecrated with shrimp and wine
The matrimony of our insatiable flesh.

I might as well annex Mississippi, too,
And name you co-trustee of my estate
That my notorious metaphors can be recorded
And more expeditiously probated
In case I predecease you.
While we're at it,
Why not initiate a class action
And extend our appropriative claims
To incorporate the entire South?
After all, carousing in the Peabody's lobby,
Who hasn't mortgaged Paradise?

Cosmic Consolations

Leaving you this glorious morning
Presents a hornèd dilemma;
Though staying one day more
Could hardly pose universal distress,
We both know I *must* get home.

Perhaps separations
Are the only protection lovers possess
Against satiety. Yet just as God
Wrested perfection from bone and flesh,
Placed yawns, sleep, and death

Between success and dreams,
Ancient and inchoate civilizations,
So too did He conceive redemption
To offset forgetfulness
By letting the human spirit refresh itself.

Lady, for now we must trust
That Predestination has taken notice of us
And made reservations in both our names
For Heaven's first available condo
Or at least a suite in the Peabody Hotel.

Changing in Midstream

Leaving the Peabody this wet Sunday morning,
My tires hiss like spider spinnerets
Weaving Beale, Gayoso, and Union Streets
Into Riverside Drive.
I gaze wistfully at Mud Island
Where Friday night and all Sabbath afternoon
We listened to black musicians
Carve niches in the sky's cathedral-like facade,
Enshrining harmonies for us to hum
Whenever revisiting this Jordan
In which our passions were baptized for life.

Mesmerized, I approach the span
I-55 traverses
Sojourning between Tennessee and Arkansas.
Recalling your futile maneuvers
To forestall our separation
With lovemaking in the strictly Southern style
Causes me to balk like a fractious mule
Sensing a snake in tall grass.
Grief-stricken, growing irrational,
Disregarding traffic,
I halt my car at the bridge's dead center

And shout out my window phrases you spoke
In your slow, whisperous Mississippi dialect
That yet echo in Memory's baffles,
Amplified by this unlikely impasse:
"98% water,
Our bodies sail on their own oceans."
"We're vessels tied to our tides."
"Bon voyage, my dear, handsome man."
I dive into your voice
And, buoyed by its siren-call drawl,
Float upstream all the way to St. Louis.

Goldenrods

This day is Jackson.
The entire afternoon is named Mississippi
In celebration of you, Lady,
Whose eyes, with subtly flirtatious winks,
Transform me and all things in nature
Into intimations of love.

Through her striated recesses
So autumnally luminous, her garden
Extending endlessly along the Natchez Trace,
We chase our shadows,
Trying to make them converge,
Engulf us in wonderment

Until all motion ceases in a field,
Just off the highway,
Filled with goldenrods so yellow
Even the sun can't compete
Or complete its rotation without blinking;
It dapples us with natural halos,

Awakens us to the creatureliness we possess,
And makes October riot our faces
With graceful smiles, bathing our skin
In liquid softness
To shimmering. We photograph each other
Against the crowded flowering,

Hoping somehow to disappear
By becoming one of those arrested moments,
Then enter the efflorescing spectrum
Eternity projects through its cosmic prism.
Tomorrow, even as I'm borne forth,
This glory-washed light

Will compel me back to you
As in a vortical, daydreamy déjà vu —
Two stems growing side by side amidst millions:
Your green eyes supple leaves;
Our vibrant, teeming love
Yellowness too yellow to fade.

Taking the Streetcar Home

Abruptly I slip from dreams, sleep, bed,
Head over heels out of love's voluptuousness
As if ascending amnesia with the bends.
Past the Capitol, over High Street,
Toward Fortification, I drive away from Us,
Then enter I-55.
Between black and sun-saturated horizon,
Jackson becomes one more bead on a rosary
Memory strokes, consoling itself:
Gluckstadt, Canton,
Pickens, Yazoo City, Grenada.

Somewhere in forenoon's corridor,
Memphis looms,
That slatternly Blanche DuBois
Whose helpless gaze, tattered lace dress
Never fail to frustrate me,
Especially when she offers me her bouquet
Of papier-mâché magnolias, wisteria,
Honeysuckle, verbena,
And dusty, blood-rust rosebuds:
Ghosts of Southern belles I've known and know,
Like the Lady I've just forsaken.

Chapter Six
VAGUE LADIES

Castrated Passion

Putting distance between myself and the City
Sets up a cause-and-effect synergy.
Despite 6 a.m.'s fog,
Slick streets, and myriad Niagaras
Cascading off the traffic,
I steadily relax
Realizing my secret is safe in fleeing's keep.
Within a matter of incremental diminishments,
My spirit enters Ste. Genevieve County;
Forgetting metamorphoses me;
I'm Limbo's "unknown soldier,"
Missouri's desert-bound Moses-poet,
Hoping to reconnect emotion's arteries and veins
To my heart's four main chambers
So that breathing freedom's sweet scents
Might lead me back through Memory
To that decade of youthful enthusiasm
Before ambition choked on its misappropriated passion.

The next five hours' drive is its own guide;
Tire rotation and side-to-side motion
Remind me I'm being kept vital
On a life-support machine, my speeding vehicle.
The miles lisp into silence;
I awaken from my flight refreshed.
The secret I've smuggled into this country
No longer requires caution.
My arrival in Mississippi inspires me
To expose those hidden desires.
Suddenly I run from my car
And, throwing off my clothes,
Go along the fence toward Rowan Oak,
Then through the entrance to Bailey's Woods
Just off Old Taylor Road.
I'm moaning, bellowing "Benjy,"
Groping for Caddy in the undergrowth,
Hoping to hold her holding me, forever.

Southern Eidolons

Pensive villager, when thy steps lead thee here
As dusky eve in fading twilight creeps
O'er this stone oh refuse not the starting tear
For her beneath this sod who sleeps.
In yonder village whence thy footsteps stray'd
Like thee she dwelt like thee with measured tread
Perchance hither oft hath come and prayed
To meet some lost one number'd with the dead.

Mary Ann

Wife of
Dr. J.R. Christian
Born at Paris, Tenn.
June 1827
Married at Holly Springs, Miss.
June 1842
And Died March 1849
in the Parish of Iberville, La.
whence at her request her
remains were removed to this
spot and deposited among a
people whom she loved so well.
She Left Two Children.
Erected by her Husband
April 1857

— Inscriptions transcribed from an obelisk in the
Hill Crest Cemetery, Holly Springs, Mississippi

Just last evening at The Warehouse
I met my newest Mississippi mistress;
We peeled and nibbled boiled Gulf shrimp
Dipped in a zesty cocktail sauce,
While sipping two tepid bottles of Mouton-Cadet

* * *

To soothe its devilish effects
Before sleeping together at loneliness' behest.
Now we're stealing away from Oxford
On this late-July afternoon.

We head easterly toward Holly Springs
So she might fulfill a proprietary desire
To include me in her entire life
By revealing maudlin childhood haunts
That apparently yet hold her,
Draw her to their immutable source,
No matter that at twenty-two
She's been gone from this village-like purlieu
For seven fugitive years.

We drive circuitously over narrow dirt roads
She knows like the creases of her palm,
Past dogtrot shacks inhabited by blacks in tatters
Who miraculously exist on lack of work,
Through desolate crossroads hamlets
Resembling "Old West" ghost-town sets,
Until we approach the outskirts —
A pecan grove, ramshackle cotton gin,
Corinthian columns still standing starkly
For the imagination to fill in with the plantation
A conflagration vanquished
Thirty years after the Civil War's conclusion.

She directs me through the center of town,
Pointing out the house where her dad reared her
As a girl (her mother, she whispers,
Eyes turned away from mine for the first time today,
Committed suicide as she turned eight —
She, like her mother, an only child,
Both loners, precocious, so she'd been told),
The double-porticoed Presbyterian church
Whose ubiquitous green steeple

* * *

➜

Scribbled the date of her confirmation in God's sky-book,
The millinery shop where she worked after school,
And the hardware store her father managed.

Suddenly we're parked beside a cast-iron fence
Whose intricate fleur-de-lis motif
Is incomplete for the ravages of weather
And vandals a hundred and fifty years deep.
We enter the Hill Crest Cemetery
And, for an indefinite hiatus,
Weave through rows of gravestones and mausoleums
Like mourning doves and barn swallows
Tilting, veering, diving,
Just above the sepulchral earth
As if waiting for a higher intellect
To decide our next direction.

Preternaturally,
And completely unconsciously,
We lose track of each other.
Finally I locate myself seated on the grass,
Knees folded, focus abstracted,
Trying to decipher the barely legible letters
Of a poem chiseled into the canted stone
In front of me, placed here
Over a century-and-a-quarter ago
By a doctor, husband, father of two,
Grieving for his twenty-two-year-old wife,
Mary Ann Christian.

For what might be an hour, century, eon,
I lapse into a pensive trance,
Oblivious of dusk seeping into late afternoon,
Touching me moistly; confusedly I awaken,
Overtaken by tears; my crying
Could be for the youthful Southern lady
Whose dust surely has dissipated

* * *

From the grave rotting beneath my gaze
Or for myself, stranded destinies from my family
Of my own dissolute volition,
Dooming myself to ruination,
A private diaspora without salvation.

But, most likely, I suddenly realize,
I've been weeping inebriated under the influence
Of the lady who's brought me here,
My most recently made companion.
My bewildered tears turn to eerie fear
That she's disappeared from this cemetery,
Somehow dematerialized, entered the twilight
As purple and pink pastel dust
Sifting into lackluster blood-rust shadows.

Before I can measure time in miles lapsed,
My solitary drive from Holly Springs
Via the highway is accomplished.
Now I'm sitting on a green, slat-backed bench
Within the broadening umbra of Oxford's Courthouse,
Witnessing ladies stroll past in cotton frocks,
Watching for some lost one
Who perchance will entrance me again this evening,
Raise me from those number'd with the dead.

Vague Lady from Holly Springs

On this cool, last afternoon in July
Whose too-blue sky
Is scribbled with cumulus hieroglyphs,
I sit on a green, wood-slatted bench
Behind a black, wrought-iron fence
Staying traffic orbiting the gray Courthouse
And, like squeezing rainbows from paint tubes,
Try to extrude palpable dreams
From these gloomy, drooping hours
To make last your rapidly disappearing
Prismatical hues.

Bribing Memory to rescent your fragrances,
I just spent three hours at lunch
Sipping tepid Mouton-Cadet,
Savoring the sweetest boiled Gulf shrimp
My tongue has tasted
Since haloing your nipples
In murmurous caress.
And even now, seeking to retrieve you,
I fix on visions of barefooted nymphs
Wearing sheer cotton frocks,
Drifting up and down Oxford's streets.

But for all my artificer's persuasiveness,
Neither my appetite nor imagination
Has provided lifelike surrogates
Capable of transubstantiating your phantom shape.
Abruptly I flee the Square
And retreat to my eucalyptus-scented room,
Where I hope to bribe sleep
To keep despair from betraying my desire
To wade nakedly
Into the pool you left in my bed at dawn
And, in your rife, wet scent, drown.

Vapors and Apparitions

Not until last evening
Had I ever perceived myself effete,
A pariah, a breathing anomaly,
And, of all things inconceivable, a liar.

But there I sat in Oxford's Warehouse,
Self-contained, writing verse,
Already into my second bottle of Mouton-Cadet,
Oblivious to raucous sounds from the lounge

Confounding the stale air around me,
Trying to ignite my dark imagination
Like a cave man striking flints
Above dank bark-shards and shavings.

Seemingly arrested in concentration's
Escape-proof Houdini box,
I fumbled with locks on image-chains,
Hoping to liberate stubborn tropes.

When I gazed up from the empty page,
She was seated, vaporous, yet mercurial,
In a space opposite my frustration —
Night's sleight of hand skillfully performed.

Ashamed in my nakedness, I squirmed;
She'd located me at the epicenter of a lie
I fabricated to avoid dining with her
To compose in isolation.

Saying, "You're not on the road heading home,"
She didn't even feign surprise
But simply lifted my filled glass to her lips,
Tongued its rim sinuously,

And drew me into her witchery.
Neither termagant, Lorelei, nor Pandora
But rather a ghostly courtesan
I'd met by chance earlier that afternoon,

➔

She forced me to compromise,
Deflect my artistic obsessiveness,
Subvert discipline's conflictive indecision
And made me crave taking her to bed.

Having intended to invent paeans to my Muses,
Beatrice, Helen, and Eloise,
I lost total control,
Fell victim to concupiscence;

As a not-quite-innocent bystander
Witnessing failure succeed,
I submitted to her victory over my spirit.
When I awakened at dawn, she was gone.

Stretched out in bed all day like a dead man,
I kept questioning not why I'd lied
But rather even tried
To resist being possessed by an eidolon.

My Heart's Darling

It's an evening of honeysuckle.
Serene Oxford can't sleep
For the obscene sweetness
Flooding town on cresting breezes.
These efflorescing summer days
Infect victims with irreversible lunacy
Like elusive recluse spiders
Biting themselves into frenzied senselessness.

Tonight, barely aware of my own diminishment,
I wander about the shimmering Square,
Then sit on a tacky Courthouse bench
And, listening to distant revelry
Spiraling like Mardi Gras serpentine
From The Warehouse restaurant,
Sift the silence for blooms
To fix in Memory's cumulative bouquet.

Unannounced, a garrulous female voice,
Lost in nonexistent conversation,
Materializes invisibly.
Through her stifled crying
She begs me to steady the tenebrous pear tree
Swaying between us
That she might scrape down, escape anonymity,
Race into my moaning loneliness,

Take my outstretched hand,
And flee from this suffocating place
To golden lands beyond Mississippi.
Turning into her naked gaze,
I witness Caddy, Quentin, Benjy,
Sister/mother, brother/lover,
All mixed up in the obscenely sweet honeysuckle,
Suddenly run from each other and from me.

It Was the Summer of the Snakes, and She Ran

It was the summer of the snakes,
And she ran nakedly down University Avenue
Instead of pacing herself through Bailey's Woods,
Running with palpitating nipples and thighs
As if to escape invisible, lacerating fangs,
Content to be gazed upon,
Violated by salacious, straining eyes,
And, accepting companionship of strangers,
Brain-raped every step she'd take.

It was the summer of the snakes,
And she ran past the Ramey-Memory House
And Buie Museum to South Lamar,
Left, then left again around the Courthouse,
A stark, wingèd, singing shape.
Malign eyes peeking from behind drapes,
Store-glass bordering the Square, warped doors,
And porches arrested her fleshy ecstasy
With a collective, accusatory stare.

It was the summer of the snakes,
And she ran from herself for her life,
Toward the pool in St. Peter's Cemetery
Where, long ago, floating in ooze,
She'd climbed up out of Youth's slime,
Simultaneously entered and been penetrated
By the great, elongated viper Time,
Her seducer, judge, and future executioner,
She his bemused, dutiful concubine.

It was the summer of the snakes,
And she ran, her demon-driven dance of death
A manifestation of her first earthly fantasy.
Entranced, almost prancing now,
Bare toes hissing atop the shifting path
Of a gliding moccasin's back,
Striding toward a nest outside Oxford,
Beyond Mississippi, skyward,
She ran . . . and she ran . . . and she ran.

Wisteria

Approaching the Missouri state line
Just miles above Blytheville,
Three hours north of Oxford,
I squirm, focus myopically
Not upon the great, white, segmented worm
Stretching endlessly ahead

But on the purple sprig of wisteria
Wilting atop the dashboard:
Ghostly Mississippi I'd picked yesterday
While visiting Rowan Oak,
Leaning against magnolias and dogwoods,
Loitering beneath her formal cedars,

Beguiled by mid-August's crystal twilight
Slipping between evergreen boughs
Scratching the sky's eyes.
I lift the twig to my mystified face,
Inhale its thick-dripping, sickly liquors;
Emily Grierson appears in the mirage they create:

No gray-haired, wizened spinster she
But ravishing mistress in crimson brocade
Waving to me even as her diaphanous shape
Continues to diminish into a past
Whose future outdistances me
No matter how urgently I keep accelerating.

Perhaps we met last night,
Dined with nothing save wine and candle-flicker
Separating our penetrating gazes,
Then made our strangers' nakedness
Shameless helpmates for ages;
Possibly it's just Chablis ethers vexing Memory.

Perplexed by her specter, I begin to suspect
Death may have visited me last evening
And that this highway I now drive
Could be her worm-infested wedding bed
Over which Mississippi's succubus hovers,
Protecting my barren spirit from grave robbery.

Chapter Seven

SEARCHING FOR THE SPICE ISLANDS

A Devotee of the Southern Way of Lovemaking

My returns to this Mississippi oasis,
Never completely calculated
Nor exactly accidental,
Are often occasioned by my insomnious imagination
That, at whim, conspires with me
To write apostrophes to Faulkner, Nature,
Caddy, Quentin, and Temple Drake
From a squeaky swivel chair in my office.
Deskbound, I circle the diurnal hours
Until, like a whirling dervish,
I emerge in the land of my fantasies.

Conversely, when visiting Mississippi,
Where naiads, dryads, and Oceanides
Assault my lusty instincts just by whispering,
Crossing the Grove barefooted,
And stretching credibility in blue jeans
Two sizes too tight,
What seems to me reality *is*,
And nothing is, except as it appears.
When here as an uninvited guest,
I'm treated respectfully,
Spared unnecessary subliminal intervention.

How convenient not needing a rationale
For surrendering to Dionysiac appetites,
Having ageless guilt absolved.
When at Ole Miss, I suspend disbelief
At the slightest drop of a pouting lip,
Twitch of an eyelid, or thigh-hitch
And accept my lesser gestures as my best.
No kingdom's Queen I might wand-conjure
And enchant with magic invocations
Could possibly approximate a Southern lady
Making herself accessible.

Rasselas

It's five o'clock Friday afternoon;
I should be arriving home by now
To celebrate with wife and children
Another work week completed.
Instead, I'm stranded in Oxford, Mississippi,
Getting blitzed sipping Chablis
By the half-carafe, disintegrating innocuously,
Integers and figments every eon,
Like Ozymandias in Time's ossuary.

What attracts and attaches me to this town
Is neither theological nor mystical,
Though both diversions might prove cathartic
For my travel-weary head and heart.
The compelling spell
Is my desire to discover in this oasis
An elixir to counteract stasis,
Relieve me of the responsibility of aging,
Going crazy growing staid.

Perhaps by exposing myself to Youth's music,
Getting high vicariously
On coke, beer, "ludes," whiskey straight, Life,
Being blown away by beauty
No Helen ever dreamed
In even the least prepossessing coed visage,
Following the mountain's upward girth
Down into the Happy Valley,
I, a shattered Rasselas,

Might undo in one night
All the vital damage done in a lifetime
Pursuing a suitable calling, writing,
Creating a decent epitaph to be carved into my stone.
Possibly the blond, tight-jeaned,
Taut-titted, submissive lady of eighteen,
Sibilantly whispering liquescent pruriences
In my heated ear, holds Freedom's secret
In her profoundly boundless evocations.

Twice her age, I writhe as her tongue
Excites my brain's penis to twice its size
Between her white, wet lips,
Then fly across iridescent rainbows
Undulating inside her dilated eyes.
Suddenly my frenzied dalliance subsides
As she gazes through my glazed inebriation
To a future friend her age
And abandons me to Fantasy's mirage.

Extravagant Fancies of an *H.M.S. Bounty* Deck Hand

Oxford is the extreme port on my clipper route
From St. Louis around the Horn
To the outer reaches of Freedom's "Known World."
Two nights adrift
And my luffing soul instinctively comes about,
Tacks homeward. "Stay awhile,
Then weigh anchor" is the formulaic refrain
My Billy Budd-blood has sung and hummed
So relentlessly for an endless decade
It no longer needs to rehearse
Before performing "spontaneous" entertainments
To crowds of one or less.

But this eve, sitting here with a half-carafe
Of platinum-tinged Chablis,
Fashioning thoughts to enter in my log,
Vague Atlantean hallucinations
Silhouette my blurred visions
With possibilities I've never conjured:
This trip — what if I didn't return,
Instead sailed for Pitcairn
To unloose new issue
In total seclusion from the adversarial world
And created an authentic language
Dependent not on phonics but touching?

What if I built a sacred hut
Dedicated to Eros, Dionysus, and Me,
Beneath whose open-air thatch
Creatures evoking primal femaleness
Might redeem me from fumbling,
A seraglio sheltering a nude harem
Whose purpose would be being discovered by me
Head to head to toes to holes
Under and above, day after night,
Allowing me to reconnect with animal origins,
Drop off intellectual vestiges,
And arouse forgotten celestial carnality?

What if? . . . What if? . . . Suddenly I shudder.
A squall from an overhead duct
Blasts my neck. Inebriation
Floods my brain's two main holds;
My ship capsizes, scuttles in a whirling pool
Not off an exotic isle
But Oxford's feculent shoals.
Come dawn, I'll have to devise ways
To raise my hulk, reckon course,
And sail home in time to escort my wife
To the annual Chamber of Commerce banquet
To receive its Man of the Year award.

Making Berth at Oxford

This is a snug harbor into which I've drifted,
Berthed ship, slipped down the gangplank,
And swaggered into Lethe unnoticed by its citizenry.

What's one more waif
When uninvited visitors endlessly descend
To pay obeisance to their patron saint, William,

Those inspired most by his prose poetry
Who know their own writing
Has been adversely affected by the "scratch"

Of that little bastard "over yonder at Oxford,"
Who, having spent his apprenticeship "Stoned,"
Exploded the mother tongue that had blown his brains?

Actually, I've "put in" this deserted Thursday
To let bids on repairs to my bowsprit,
Have the foresail mended and refitted with battens,

The main halyards replaced by a hemp-weaver,
Not go crazy fornicating in St. Peter's
With female ghosts flying low enough to lay,

Whose surnames might also happen to be Faulkner.
I could care less whether they worship
White writer, "nigra," old-world Jew,

Or one-legged navigator like me, A(ha)b Snopes.
My first and only concern is *my* survival,
Not someone else's posthumous apotheosis.

As soon as my vessel is seaworthy,
I'll set sail in quest of bleached whales
Whose enormity besieges me with wonderment.

Tonight, confined to this leeward harbor,
I'll likely bow without grace to base complacence,
Exercise my least attractive appetites,

Locate available "snatch," as Mr. Bill might say,
And partake of the nightly sound-and-light show
Beginning at nine, lingering past dawn.

Laid up indeterminately,
Waiting for parts to outfit my distressed spirit,
I may as well sample Oxford's exotic spices.

Just now, a native eyeing me shyly
Comes into irons, drops anchor alongside.
Admittedly intrigued by my gimp leg,

She brazens our gam with beguilements.
Knowing sirens can't resist stranded sailors,
I ignore her whorish blandishments — for two seconds.

On the Virtues of Being a Man of Action

Passionate actions may not last long
Nor reveal their perpetrator
As one possessing the quintessence of class
Or motivated by selflessness,
But they certainly suggest spontaneous energy
Effectively arrested
And focused to accomplish the necessary climax
Between the animal in question
And the object of his licentious affections.

In layman's nomenclature, what this signifies
Is that a fella with Rabelaisian appetites
Either shits or gets into the pot,
No fucking around.
Getting R.I.P.ed is to drown in the Now
That liquor and drugs power,
To "die" in the sense of getting laid
As the Avon bard implied in his persuasions to love
When he intended to swell the sexual progress of a play.

It's uninhibited exhibitionism to the max,
Tomorrow today, right this very eon,
Despite the Einsteinian time-lag
Inherent in straight lines that bend convention
Whenever mores bore younger generations
And die of spiritual attrition.
It's Emmett Kelly sweeping dinosaur dung
Under the Vatican's Gobelin tapestries
Just because it's a *gas* to hide the Truth.

It's Hemingway breaking fast
At his own last movable feast in Idaho,
Not even inviting God to partake of his *Kiddush*
By shattering his shot glass
After toasting Senility and Cowardice;
It's Faulkner making one more drunk jump
Before being thrown from Bergson's horse
Into a paraldehyde stream of consciousness
Flowing through Byhalia, Mississippi.

In the short run, much praise should be accorded
The Perpetrator of Passionate Actions,
Who doesn't hesitate to fight an oversized opponent
And instinctively knows how to equalize odds,
Get even by getting stoned
Before kneeing Goliath in his gonads,
Exacting from Cyclops an eye for an eye,
And make Death a believer
That Life doesn't survive by sitting on its ass.

Earthly Rewards

Yet another trip; this time from Helena:
I navigate its Mississippi River bridge,
A wide anxiety for this outsider,
And sail a 12-mile Delta stretch,
The first leg on the zigzag voyage
Taking me south to Clarksdale,
Then east through Marks and Batesville
And on into Oxford by late afternoon.

Volume blasting, I play Randy Newman's
L.A. "blues" on tape
To get in the mood for concupiscence.
Allusions to "Kingfish" Huey,
Herbert Hoover, Lester Maddox, rednecks,
East St. Louis, Birmin'ham,
And the "Keepin' the niggers down" refrain
Grate up my reclining spine,

Remind me I'm a pirate in disguise,
Come uninvited to the university
Forty miles from Jefferson
To wile away a night as troubadour
With ledger book, phoenix-quill pen, wine,
Sporting a careless arrogance
And profligate insularity
Befitting the self-imposed Bohemian image

I must have "cottoned to" in youth
(That studiously unstudied derring-do
Hemingway feigned in his San Fermín daze,
Scott and Zelda affected
Splashing half-naked in their *Plaza* de Torsos).
Hoping to sculpt from one wet-clay night
A shape resembling Michelangelo's David
With words and licentiousness,

I fail to achieve such noble accomplishments
For lack of spontaneity.
Instead, I sit on my fat ass all evening
Swigging chilled Chablis
From half-carafes repeatedly drawn
And charged to a growing tab,
Ogling the slender feline physique
And seductive coed face

Of every effete Caddy Compson
In Oxford's Warehouse Restaurant
Where I've cast my lot
To write odes to Mankind,
Womanhood, Fellowship, Love
(Angelic, courtly, pastoral, erotic),
Melancholy Politics, Youth and Age,
Day and Night, Life and Death,

Without hierarchical priority.
Dejectedly, as my ledger pages fill
With soaring, swill-brained metaphors,
Oblique visions, and dissonant riffs,
I'm reminded that a writer's life,
Of absolute necessity,
Is a matter of sacrificing action
For a little thought, a bit of scribbling,

And one shitpot load of being lonely
No matter the spirit's locus.
Before I know it, one o'clock and I
Are the only cronies left in this bar.
I pay, weave to the hotel in my car,
Read the note taped to my door,
My place, Temple, and hastily about-face,
My faith renewed — Art do take care of its own!

Chapter Eight

GOAT-POET

Sir Galwyn of Arthgyl

Without the slightest tip of my hat to Time,
I've arrived, faith's leap from Missouri
Through Arkansas and Tennessee into Mississippi
Performed in the wink of an eye;
My artificer's mind blinks
Simply by aiming its necromantic ink
In legible script across doomsday pages
My breathing inspires on mystical cue.

First to recognize me are loblolly pines
Lining I-55, which guides me home to Oxford
Via Sardis, Senatobia, Water Valley,
Batesville, Como, and Holly Springs;
Singing a pleasing litany this glistening morning,
Each is a naked, surrogate mistress
Bestowing on my lusty senses
Temptation capable of making exultation happen.

By this evening, I'll have surrendered
To magical aphrodisiacs,
Tasted the sweetest female delicacies,
Become slave to excesses so titillating
To refuse indulging them would undo the philter,
Render me a shorn ewe-nuch
Not rabidly passionate cloven-hoofed goat,
Lotus-eater conspicuously concupiscent.

No! No! One must never abstain
From reprobate vagrancies, evanescent dalliances
Nor refrain from spontaneous licentiousness,
Provided these occasions are discreetly immoral.
Tonight, to libidinize my vital spirit,
Rather than fantasizing, I'll dance on a grave,
Consort with courtesans *and* ghosts,
And fornicate with Mississippi's hornèd moon.

The Warehouse: Friday Night

The smooth, cool, intoxicating wine I sip
Slips soothingly down my throat,
Flows into my brain; wilted mind-vines inflate.
Wisteria, honeysuckle, crape myrtle,
Magnolia, lilac, and bougainvillea glisten,
Grow profusely in my informal gardens.
I sit back witnessing Chablis-rain,
Inspired by ripe grape libation
Cluster-plucked, squeezed, fermented in my arbor,
Rejuvenate the desolate crescent
I converted into a desert metaphors ago.

The civilization amidst which I repose
This Friday night is Mississippi:
Neither Indian nor "Scotrish"
But homogeneous chauvinist Male
Suckling America's robust coed breasts.
Every day in this red-clay plain,
Named Oxford, with a modicum of satanic wit,
Is Friday night, "show time,"
Roy Scheider popping uppers, getting laid
For the sake of saving face with an avowed feminist,
La Belle Dame Sans Merci.

Tonight, orthodox Jews observe Sabbath:
For my lonely spirit,
An excommunicated, secular renegade from the faith,
This evening marks the End's onset,
The beginning of physical apocalypse;
My psyche drowns in a wine-shower
Eclipsing the gibbous moon.
Abruptly I postpone my cynicism
To concentrate on the animated face of May Melton,
Tonight's Moulin Rouge lady,
Imbibing, smoking, posing across the way.

I die a thousand births in a solitary sigh.
Imagining myself twenty years younger,
Fucking flowering Judas trees, succulents,
Venus' flytraps, birds-of-paradise —
Ole Miss varieties
Tended by sissified boys and effeminate men,
Who seed, graft, and repot them frequently
To procreate, in hothouse slumber,
Grail-children identical in size, pattern, hue —
I devour her fleshy Lautrec wink,
Hoping she'll share my hydroponic bed.

The Profligate

Pac-Man's agitated demons
Parade beneath the glass
Separating me from their programmed display
In this raucous drinking place.

I try to locate my dissociated soul
Amidst the buxom college ladies
Sauntering in and out, try to decide
Why my base intentions are so primed tonight;

I'm neither waiting for an old acquaintance
Nor anticipating
Someone I've not met before;
In truth, I'd prefer purchasing a whore

To defuse my inordinate energy.
Instead, having consumed two half-carafes
Of chilled Chablis, I withstand
A garrulous law student's inane conversation

And, as he notches martini after dry martini
On his sedentary butt,
Endure his antic improvisations
Competing with Willie Nelson, Conway Twitty,

Kenny Rogers, and Barbara Mandrell,
Darling of the college circuit,
Even in this most pretentious,
Least "country" center of the Confederacy,

Ole Miss. I gaze about this room,
Amused by the blatant mating rites
Homo sapiens invents,
Then sink back into my own private delusions

To focus on copulating with a female
Capable of healing my ailing libido,
Willing to minister to my dissipations
Without expectation of recompense or lasting commitments

Just for the opportunity to be "of service"
To someone who could use a dose of affection.
Abruptly I grope for the men's room,
Hoping to regain my equilibrium.

In the hallway, Temple Drake pinches my rear;
Ass-essing her vulnerability,
I suggest she let me whisk her to the hotel
Where I'm living tonight.

I piss in my pants on the way.
The rest is history: Success! Eureka!
Fucking is definitely failure's best remedy.
Look how healthy I've grown!

Cloven-Hoofed Goat

They flock to this place, The Warehouse,
To get tipsy, crocked, wasted,
Go home in a totally devastated craziness
With anyone willing to pay attention.

I, a pariah, witness the continuous charade,
This parade of Vestal Virgins
Submitting themselves as nocturnal oblations
To the most propitious accidental gods,

Knowing that the ultimate consequence,
After infatuation and pregnancy, is marriage;
A mildly shameful education
By which procreation perpetuates itself.

As I sit here, witnessing the influx,
Intimations of the goat-footed satyr predominate;
I begin to doubt my efficacy
As a writer, lover, sipper of chilled Chablis.

Suddenly three wayward females
Confront and force me to identify myself;
My Jewish features have piqued them;
The bulge in my unpleated pants

Intrigues and brings them to my knees
Begging to be admitted into my private demesne.
Slowly I lower the drawbridge,
Raise the portcullis; they titter,

Then enter. The wine grows sweeter,
Thicker; my words slur
In vertiginous circles as we step closer
To that moment when two will retreat

Leaving just us to maneuver
Toward conclusive human confusion
Neither will refuse — a perfect excuse
To submit our impersonal souls

To review by a stranger. But, unexpectedly,
Gazing into her reflective eyes,
I see a gargoyle with my features leering at me,
Its flicking asp's tongue lacerating my face.

Goat-poet's Agony

Dwindling day is a Mouton-Cadet bouquet
Escaping behind a released cork
From afternoon's moist, smoothly contoured neck
Into lilac twilight. I sip its essence
As if lips, buds, and brain cells
Had never tasted such fresh female fragrances;

Those rife odors of frantic honeysuckle,
Bee-bothered, sweet as pea pods
Sucked clean, clammy as ewe teats
Throbbing from young, rough tongues,
And redbud, althea, magnolia, cedar, and spirea,
Exploding into Fourth of July girandoles
Across Autumn's horizon, agitate me;
I grow intoxicated on Oxford's nocturnal vapors.

Suddenly a slave to hallucinatory vagrancies,
A dislocated ghost groping homeward,
I tear off my clothes, run nakedly
Past the kudzu-cloyed railroad cut,
Down Old Taylor Road toward Bypass #6.
Entering pastel dusk's labial gates,

Penetrating night's densely suspended membranes,
My impregnated heart's pulse convulses,
Finally subsides to that of a hibernating bear.
Eons liquidize before I awaken
From bittersweet dream-sleep crowded with demons
Who masturbated my flaccid penis
Into a bloated ego, then crowned me
Exalted Imperial Wizard of Mississippi Klaverns.

Possessed by nervous energy,
I resist their oppressive threats, keep running
As if fear were no mere pathetic fallacy,
Instead existed as a physical nemesis
To be outdistanced despite its psychic pain.
But blood clots in my thighs; I hyperventilate.

Night leers perniciously,
Sneers at its unclothed victim,
Snared like a scared human gyved to a shore
By horrified Lilliputians. "It's all a mistake,"
I proclaim to the oblivious gibbous moon.
"I'm innocent. Can't you see?
Being and being here were *Actsidents* of God.
I had no choice. Don't you see?

"Leave me Be, you Fuck!
I mean you no harm;
I simply strayed too far from home,
And loneliness overtook me in the Doldrums
Three hundred thirty-three miles
South by Southeast in No-Man's latitudes

Where I allowed sensibility to spend itself
Savoring a dwindling Mississippi day
Instead of remembering that poets
Aren't pimps for metaphors hitchhiking to Oblivion."
Disillusioned, I watch Oxford's fascination fade,
That which once drew me insatiably to its mystic bouquet,
And its liquors ferment into vinegar.
Stuporous, I toast the lunatic Moon's collapse.

One Last Crusade to Oxford

After three months of the sweetest inactivity,
The road-queen, whore Lorelei,
Tempts me from my self-proclaimed "priesthood,"
Beguiles me onto I-55 again.

Going south, gazing into a sun-glazed daze,
My crazy-quilted senses alternate
Between a fumbling, narcoleptic dance of death
And stunning orgasm; my mind collapses.

I can't remember massaging a smoother back,
Manipulating more pliant vertebrae
Than these this sensual road offers me today,
Nor have metaphors come more fluidly.

Sliding silently down her spine toward Memphis,
Visions of her cunt beneath my body,
Seething with semen-seeds,
Not Winter's frigid flesh,

Set up such unexpected frustration
My groin explodes, freezes inside its own heat.
By degrees, my lust crusts over,
Leaves me stranded on a polar floe

Slowly dissolving below afternoon's blaze,
Going rapidly nowhere,
Lapsing between monastic abstinence
And ejaculative rites of passage.

After my drive to Oxford and back has climaxed,
I'll be asking myself why you, Lorelei,
Selected me on whom to practice your rhythm method
And satisfy your oversexed drive —

Could it have been your vixenish debauchery
Taunting my listless existence out of hiding
Or your haunting Isadora death wish
Flaunting its siren perniciousness,

Insinuating my penitential spirit
With echoes of that reprobate decade
When Youth took to the road hellbent
And never spent a night alone in the "Styx"?

Driving south now, I already know how
On my return Crusade,
I'll pray God keeps me from wrecking
And lets me, though defeated, reach St. Louis

And how, groping to express my guilt,
I'll make my devotional sign of the Cross,
This middle finger, stick it out the window,
And shout, "Up Yours, Bitch," all the way home.

Caving In

Heading south to rendezvous with noon,
My fleeing spirit peers inward
Through terraqueous caverns
For an exit into future hours
Backing up on themselves;
An orange-gray, mist-laden horizon,
Split as if into cosmic firmaments, shimmers,
Its slanted rays stalactites
Dripping from God's ceiling into my eyes.
I'm a blind, black amphibian
Swimming in fifty fathoms of opaque confusion.

Until now, whether above ground or beneath,
The location of my oneiric psyche
Has seemed no more than a hysterical shriek
From Bedlam's porch, Pandemonium's gate.
Heading toward Memphis, Oxford,
I sense my soul ascending the cave,
Being penetrated by vague benedictions
Emanating from angels haloing my passage
From Sleep to Freedom's source.
As the light at tunnel's end intensifies,
I enter its glow — Mississippi draws me home.

A Day of Reckoning

Slowly, my hibernating soul shudders,
Gasps for breath, stirs, stretches,
Stares through bare spaces in the cave
Amnesia has trenched a decade deep
Beneath my physical existence.

Perhaps a fragrant trace of honeysuckle,
Overripe magnolia, or wisteria
Circulating through my bloodstream
Has awakened sleepy spirits and ghosts
From their enchanted Van Winkledom.

Possibly a wayward cloud
Diaphanously draped, curvaceously shaped,
Like a vague lady from Holly Springs
Whose naked flesh and intellect
Once saved me from lunacy, excites me now

By its sheer, supple hovering above vision,
Its untouched simplicity, its freedom
Just to ornament the moment; nothing more!
Maybe the reverberation of tires
Grazing the highway's glistening pavement,

Setting up a paradisal reiteration,
Has motivated my bones to locate a frequency
On which they might realign themselves
With notes flowing down from God's throat
Into Bailey's Woods' cathedral.

Possibly this resurrection may just be
My ultimate overcoming of drag coefficients,
Achieving that necessary lift
The spirit hopes to catch as it rotates,
Assumes "homing" altitude.

Whatever natural explanations
I might piece together to render rational
My absolutely miraculous rising from the cave,
I, an anti-Christ, vow beyond a "shadow"
I'll never chase another slatternly yawn.

Epilogue

Pan Damned

Persistent yet intermittent visions of you,
Belle Mississippi,
Twist inextricably amidst my psyche's leaves
And velvety dripping poetries
Like sinuous, thick-scented honeysuckle vines
Trying to break free from Quentin's pent-up mind
And stretch their lunatic blooms moonward.

But like half-chewed carrots,
They lodge in my throat; I choke.
Memories of Southern ladies I've intimately known
All respond to the same name
When I call them, Caddy. Spoken to,
Mississippi coalesces into the solitary specter
Of a hydra-headed Medusa hissing at me.

Momentarily, daily, year after year,
I float belly-up on nightmarish oceans
As if my mother were a fish
And I her amniotic death wish delivered,
A speck whose minuscule history
Is this visionary obituary written in verse.
Why did I ever worship you, bitch, Mississippi?

Louis Daniel Brodsky was born in St. Louis, Missouri, in 1941, where he attended St. Louis Country Day School. After earning a B.A., Magna Cum Laude, at Yale University in 1963, he received an M.A. in English from Washington University in 1967 and an M.A. in Creative Writing from San Francisco State University the following year.

From 1968 until 1987, while maintaining his poetry writing schedule, he managed a 350-person men's clothing factory and developed a chain of "Slack Outlets" for Biltwell Co., Inc. of St. Louis, Missouri.

Mr. Brodsky is the author of sixteen volumes of poetry. In addition, he has published eight scholarly books on Nobel laureate William Faulkner, and most recently, a biography titled **William Faulkner, Life Glimpses**.

Also available from **Time Being Books**

LOUIS DANIEL BRODSKY
You Can't Go Back, Exactly
The Thorough Earth
Four and Twenty Blackbirds Soaring
Mississippi Vistas: Volume One of *A Mississippi Trilogy*
Forever, for Now: Poems for a Later Love
A Gleam in the Eye: Poems for a First Baby

WILLIAM HEYEN
Pterodactyl Rose: Poems of Ecology
Erika: Poems of the Holocaust
Ribbons: The Gulf War — A Poem

LOUIS DANIEL BRODSKY and WILLIAM HEYEN
Falling from Heaven: Holocaust Poems of a Jew and a Gentile

Please call or write for a free catalog.

TIME BEING BOOKS
POETRY IN SIGHT AND SOUND
Saint Louis, Missouri

10411 Clayton Road • Suites 201-203
St. Louis, Missouri 63131
(314) 432-1771

TO ORDER TOLL-FREE
(800) 331-6605 Monday through Friday, 8 a.m. to 4 p.m. Central time
FAX: (314) 432-7939